W9-BVP-987

ENIGMAS *of* HISTORY

THE MYSTERY OF TUTANKHAMUN

WORLD
BOOK

a Scott Fetzer company

Chicago

www.worldbook.com

World Book edition of "Enigmas de la historia" by Editorial Sol 90.

Enigmas de la historia
La tumba de Tutankamón

This edition licensed from Editorial Sol 90 S.L.
Copyright 2013 Editorial Sol S.L. All rights reserved.

Revised printing, 2016
English-language revised edition copyright 2015
World Book, Inc.
Enigmas of History
The Mystery of Tutankhamun

World Book, Inc.
180 North LaSalle Street
Suite 900
Chicago, Illinois 60601
USA

For information about other World Book publications,
visit our website at **www.worldbook.com** or call
1-800-967-5325.

Library of Congress Cataloging-in-Publication Data

Tumba de Tutankamón. English.
  The mystery of Tutankhamun. -- English-language
revised edition.
      pages cm. -- (Enigmas of history)
   Summary: "An exploration of the questions and mysteries surrounding the pharaoh Tutankhamun. Feat
ures include, fact boxes, biographies of famous experts
on ancient Egypt, places to see and visit, a glossary,
further readings, and index"--Provided by publisher.
English translation of La tumba de Tutankamón,
published 2013 by Editorial Sol S.L.
  Includes index.
  ISBN 978-0-7166-2678-7

  1. Tutankhamen, King of Egypt--Juvenile literature.
2. Egypt--Civilization--To 332 B.C.--Juvenile literature. I. World Book, Inc. II. Title. III. Series: Enigmas
of history.
DT87.5.T7413 2015
932'.014092--dc23
                                        2015009315

Enigmas of History Set ISBN: 978-0-7166-2670-1

Printed in China by Shenzhen Donnelley
Printing Co., Ltd., Guangdong Province
2nd printing June 2016

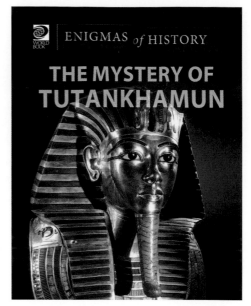

The golden funerary mask that covered the face
of Tutankhamun's mummified body.

© Werner Forman/Topham/The Image Works

Staff

Glossary There is a glossary of terms on page 44. Terms defined in the glossary are in boldface **(type that looks like this)** on their first appearance on any *spread* (two facing pages). Words that are difficult to say are followed by a pronunciation (pruh NUHN see AY shuhn) the first time they are mentioned.

Contents

Rediscovering Tutankhamun

In November 1922, a British *archaeologist* (scientist who studies the remains of past human cultures), Howard Carter, discovered something fantastic among the desert cliffs of Upper Egypt—the southern region along the Nile River. There, Carter discovered the sealed tomb of the ancient king Tutankhamun. Tutankhamun's tomb lay in the Valley of the Kings, so-called because of the valley's many ancient Egyptian royal tombs. The ancient Egyptians buried their kings and queens in elaborate tombs packed with objects to be used in the afterlife, including precious oils, weapons, and furniture, as well as gold, jewels, and other riches. Over time, thieves discovered and plundered many of the tombs.

Tutankhamun's tomb, however, lay hidden by rubble and largely undisturbed since the time of his burial more than 3,300 years ago. Howard Carter opened the tomb to find a collection of more than 5,000 objects, including Tutankhamun's mummified remains and vast amounts of gold—the "flesh of the gods" in ancient Egypt. Egyptians considered the king, or pharaoh, a god and the son of a god.

Tutankhamun (sometimes spelled *Tutankhamen*) became king of Egypt as a young boy. He ruled from about 1332 B.C. until his death—aged just 18 or 19—around 1322 B.C. His reign was brief, and he was largely forgotten by history. But Carter's discovery made Tutankhamun—today often called *Tut* or *King Tut*—ancient Egypt's most famous king.

Carter, who had worked in the Egyptian deserts since 1891, had been looking for Tutankhamun for years. The rulers from Egypt's New Kingdom (1545-1075 B.C.) were buried in the Valley of the Kings, and Tutankhamun's tomb was the only one that had not been found. Carter—and many other archaeologists and treasure hunters—thought there was a chance Tutankhamun's tomb might be found *intact* (with nothing missing). If so, the tomb promised unimaginable riches.

In 1907, an archaeological team led by American Theodore M. Davis found a pit containing items marked with Tutankhamun's name. Davis believed the pit was what remained of the king's tomb, and that the items were all that remained of his riches. Everyone gave up the search for Tutankhamun—except for Carter. He was convinced the tomb had yet to be found.

The outbreak of World War I (1914-1918) interrupted and delayed Carter's quest, but he resumed his work in the Valley of the Kings near the end of the war. He and his team found little of importance until 1922, when they noticed a stone step near the well-known tomb of Ramses VI, a pharaoh who ruled nearly 200 years after Tutankhamun.

Digging through layers of sand and rubble, Carter followed the stone step down to another, and another. Sixteen steps led to a plaster door stamped with the royal seal of Tutankhamun. Thrilled, Carter summoned his financial sponsor, a British nobleman and amateur **Egyptologist** named Lord Carnarvon, to Egypt. Carnarvon soon joined Carter, who broke through the plaster door to find heaps of rubble before a second door. On Nov. 26, 1922, Carter knocked a hole in the second door and thrust a candle into the darkness on the other side. Lord Carnarvon anxiously asked, "Can you see anything?" "Yes," Carter famously replied in amazement, "wonderful things!" Carter had found the intact tomb of Tutankhamun.

The discovery brought Carter and Carnarvon quick fame, but Carnarvon became ill and died a few months later. His death and the untimely deaths of others involved with the discovery led to popular belief in a "pharaoh's curse." Newspapers popularized the legend, but Carter, who lived until 1939, dismissed the curse as superstitious nonsense. Still, the legend never died.

The most important find in the tomb was Tutankhamun himself. His preserved body, or **mummy**, lay in a solid gold coffin. Near him in the tomb were the two small, sad mummies of his children who died before they were born.

The discovery of Tutankhamun's intact tomb was the most famous and one of the most significant archaeological finds in modern history. The **artifacts** brought much detail to the life of a nearly forgotten ancient Egyptian king. They also provided a rare glimpse at the rich beliefs of the ancient **civilization.** But the tomb and its contents created as many questions as they answered. The tomb was small, much smaller than other royal tombs, and its decorations were much simpler. Why? Who exactly was Tutankhamun, and how, or why, did he die so young? Was his burial rushed? Examinations of his mummy show that he suffered from ailments that included birth defects, malaria, and probably *epilepsy* (a brain disorder). He also suffered a broken leg above the knee, an injury that could have become infected and killed him. But how did the injury occur? Some historians speculate that Tutankhamun, who lived in a time of great upheaval in Egypt, was murdered.

Tutankhamun's tomb provided some of civilization's greatest artistic treasures. Today, Tutankhamun, his treasures, and his mysteries continue to fascinate people more than 3,300 years after his death.

ROYAL CHAMBERS
The dark entrance to Tutankhamun's tomb (center) lies in the harsh terrain of the Valley of the Kings. It is surrounded by entrances to other tombs.

The Pathway to Tutankhamun

For more than 3,000 years, the body of Tutankhamun lay in its dark and silent tomb beneath the sands of Egypt. In the 1800's, a series of events led to the eventual "resurrection" of the Egyptian pharaoh in 1922.

Italian adventurer Giovanni Battista Belzoni (1778-1823) was an **archaeologist,** engineer, explorer, and circus strong man. In 1815, the "Great Belzoni" (as he called himself) took a job with the British consul in Egypt, Henry Salt. A collector of *antiquities* (ancient objects), Salt sent Belzoni to Thebes in Upper Egypt to retrieve the 7.25-ton (6.6-metric ton) bust of Ramses II, the most celebrated king of ancient Egypt. Belzoni headed a team that dragged the giant granite statue to the Nile River, where it was put on a boat and sent to London. Belzoni—like so many others hypnotized by the wonders of ancient Egypt—removed an *obelisk* (tall, four-sided stone column) from the Nile island temple of Philae and discovered the exquisite tomb of Seti I (sometimes called "Belzoni's tomb") in the Valley of the Kings. He went south to excavate the temples of Abu Simbel, each with its own giant statues of Ramses II. In 1818, Belzoni found the hidden entrance to the **pyramid** of Khafre at Giza. In 1821, he recreated Seti's tomb for the Egyptian Hall exhibition in London.

Belzoni collected numerous antiquities, and he wrote extensively about his travels. His written works fascinated the world and helped popularize *Egyptology* (study of the culture of Ancient Egypt). Future generations, including a young Howard Carter, read of his adventures and dreamed of going to Egypt themselves. Belzoni saved many Egyptian monuments and **artifacts,** but his methods were crude by today's standards, and many ancient items he handled were damaged or destroyed.

READ LIKE AN EGYPTIAN

For many centuries, people had tried and failed to understand the written language of ancient Egyptian **hieroglyphics.** A breakthrough occurred in 1799, however, when a French army officer discovered an ancient translation stone near the Lower Egyptian (northern) town of Rosetta. The so-called "Rosetta Stone" featured a text repeated in Greek, hieroglyphics, and **demotic,** a more modern form of the Egyptian written language. The stone's discovery proved to be one of the most important archaeological finds in history.

French scholar Jean-François Champollion (1790-1832) had been fascinated by ancient Egypt since he was a young boy. He took up the challenge of the Rosetta Stone by comparing the stone's different texts. After painstaking study, Champollion figured out that hieroglyphic symbols often represented **phonetic** sounds just like the letters of the alphabet. Before long, he became the first modern person to understand Egyptian hieroglyphics. In 1828, Champollion began a much-publicized tour of Egypt, where he read hieroglyphics like an ancient Egyptian!

Champollion changed the world's understanding of ancient Egypt overnight. Suddenly, people could read the many thousands of ancient texts carved into stone, painted on artifacts, or written on **papyrus scrolls.** Egyptian names, dates, and events became clear. Champollion soon toured the known tombs of the Valley of the Kings, declaring it to be the royal *necropolis* (city devoted to tombs and burial) of ancient Egypt's New Kingdom.

PRICELESS TREASURE
The flawless, golden *funerary* (burial) mask of Tutankhamun was the most outstanding piece found in his tomb.

EGYPTOMANIA

In the decades after Champollion *deciphered* (translated) Egyptian **hieroglyphics,** hundreds of ancient sites were discovered up and down the Nile. Reading the texts from the sites, **archaeologists** created an accurate list of the monarchs of ancient Egypt. They also knew—generally—where the kings and queens were buried. Tomb after tomb was found, but, over thousands of years, each one had been largely robbed of its contents. Still, the finds were remarkable and profitable, as well as popular. Egyptomania swept through Europe and America, and thousands of tourists arrived to see the **pyramids** and tombs. The tourists, however, nearly always went home with ancient **artifacts.** Nations, too, joined in the plunder, as **obelisks** and other large artifacts (such as Belzoni's bust of Ramses II) were uprooted and replanted in London, Paris, New York, and other world cities. Archaeologists doubled their efforts, hoping to find and protect Egyptian artifacts and monuments.

THE AMARNA LETTERS

In 1887, ancient clay tablets were discovered in the Middle Egypt village of Amarna. Many of the tablets, inscribed in **cuneiform** *Akkadian* (an ancient language from nearby **Mesopotamia**), proved to be letters from foreign kings to Amenhotep IV, who ruled Egypt from 1353 to 1336 B.C. The letters confirmed that Amarna was the site of the great capital city Akhetaten.

Amenhotep IV was Tutankhamun's father. In the fifth year of his reign, Amenhotep underwent a significant religious conversion, devoting himself to just one **deity,** the sun god Aten. He abandoned the state religion of many gods led by the powerful Amun, the patron god of Thebes (present-day Luxor), the royal capital in Upper Egypt. He changed his name from Amenhotep, meaning *Amun is Pleased*, to Akhenaten, or *Servant of Aten*. He also moved the capital from Thebes some 250 miles (400 kilometers) north to present-day Amarna.

WIFE AND SISTER

Tutankhamun and his wife Ankhesenamun appear on this **relief** from the back of the king's golden throne. Ankhesenamun was Tutankhamun's half-sister. Royal families *intermarried* (married close family members) to keep governing power within the bloodline.

KING TUT

Howard Carter (above right, kneeling) studies Tutankhamun's **sarcophagus** in 1924. Of all the riches Carter found in the tomb, none touched him as deeply as finding the pharaoh himself.

He called the new capital Akhetaten, meaning *Horizon of Aten*.

Tutankhamun, meaning *Living Image of Amun*, was originally named Tutankhaten, or *Living Image of Aten*. His father died when he was still a young boy. The royal advisors and priests—most of whom had lost power during Akhenaten's reign—reinstated the old gods, renamed the boy pharaoh, and moved the capital back to Thebes. Later leaders destroyed the city of Akhetaten and did their best to erase Akhenaten's name from history.

Among the archaeologists who excavated and helped explain the mysteries of Amarna were the Italian Alessandro Barsanti (1858–1917), Flinders Petrie (1853–1942) of the United Kingdom, and Howard Carter (1874-1939).

THE VALLEY OF THE KINGS

With the notable exception of Akhenaten (whose tomb is at Amarna), Egyptian rulers of the New Kingdom were buried across the Nile from Thebes in the Valley of the Kings. The New Kingdom included 32 monarchs from three **dynasties** over a period of some 500 years. By the time Carter arrived in 1891, more than two dozen tombs—belonging to kings as well as lesser nobles—had been found in the valley. Carter worked as an illustrator and surveyor for Flinders Petrie before becoming an archaeologist himself. Carter also worked with French archaeologist Édouard Naville (1844-1926), whose excavations included the remarkable Temple of Hatshepsut—a woman pharaoh of the New Kingdom.

French **Egyptologist** Gaston Maspero (1846-1916), chief of the Egyptian Antiquities Service, hired Carter as an inspector in 1899. In the following years, Carter oversaw the discovery of several new tombs in the Valley of the Kings. Carter supervised digs for Theodore M. Davis (1837-1915) and others before leaving the service in 1905. In 1907, Carter was hired by George Herbert, Lord Carnarvon (1866-1923). Carnarvon and Carter made several minor discoveries, but they shared one ultimate goal: finding the tomb of Tutankhamun.

THE BOY PHARAOH EMERGES

By 1914, 61 tombs had been found in the Valley of the Kings. Theodore Davis's teams had found a number of them, but, after many years of searching, Davis believed the area contained no more tombs. Tired and ailing, Davis, who owned the only permit to excavate in the Valley of the Kings, left Egypt. Carnarvon took over Davis's permit, but World War I (1914-1918) interrupted work in the area for years.

Carter returned to the Valley of the Kings in 1917. He knew Davis had found objects related to Tutankhamun, and he concentrated his efforts on nearby unexcavated areas. For years, he methodically removed large amounts of sand and rubble, but he found little of importance.

In the summer of 1922, Lord Carnarvon summoned Carter to the United Kingdom. He had decided to give up the search for Tutankhamun. Carnarvon's health was poor, and, after years of financing the work in Egypt, his money was running low. Carter insisted on continuing the search, offering to pay for it himself. Convinced by Carter's dedication

and enthusiasm, Carnarvon decided to give it one last try. He would finance a final season of excavation that autumn and winter.

By November 1922, Carter's operation was back in full swing in the Valley of the Kings. On November 4, amid the ruins of ancient workmen's huts near the tomb of Ramses VI, a stone step was revealed. Carter cleared the step and realized it was the beginning of a staircase leading down into the hillside. After clearing 16 steps, Carter arrived at a sealed door. Cutting a small hole in the door, he saw a passage filled with debris. Excited, Carter resisted the massive temptation to keep working. This was officially Carnarvon's dig, and, if the door did indeed lead to Tut's tomb, he wanted Carnarvon to be there when they opened it.

Carter ordered the entrance closed and replaced the excavated material. He sent a telegram to Lord Carnarvon in the United Kingdom: "At last have made wonderful discovery in valley; a magnificent tomb with seals intact; recovered same for your arrival; congratulations."

Returning to the site, Carter found what he was looking for on the sealed door: the royal stamp of Tutankhamun. However, he also found signs of tampering; someone had been there before. Beyond the door, Carter's team cleared debris from a small room only to find a second door. This door also bore the royal stamp of Tutankhamun, but it too showed signs of previous entry.

Lord Carnarvon arrived in Egypt and, on November 26, he stood with Carter before the second sealed door. Using a small chisel, Carter dug a hole in the plaster door. The heated air of many centuries breathed through the hole. Holding a candle, Carter thrust

W. M. Flinders Petrie
(1853-1942)

In 1880, British **archaeologist** Flinders Petrie began a series of mappings and digs in Egypt that resulted in a number of important discoveries. Self-educated, Petrie served as professor of Egyptology at University College, London, from 1892 to 1933. His work at Amarna—with Howard Carter—helped fill in the background story of Tutankhamun. It also created Carter's fascination with the boy king.

METHODS Many of Petrie's excavation and object-dating techniques are still in use today.

Harry Burton
(1879-1940)

Howard Carter hired esteemed British photographer Harry Burton to record Tutankhamun's tomb on film. Burton's 1,400 photographs of the tomb and its contents are among the best works of archaeological photography in history.

DOCUMENTATION Burton spent eight years photographing and filming the treasures of Tutankhamun.

Howard Carter (1874-1939)

Like many archaeologists of his day, Howard Carter learned his trade in the field. His fascination with ancient Egypt took him to Beni Hassan in Middle Egypt, where he began his career as an illustrator at just 17. A talented artist, he worked as a *tracer*, copying drawings and texts on paper for later study. He also made sketches and watercolors of ancient Egyptian art, monuments, and tombs. Carter learned archaeology from the highly regarded Flinders Petrie and other established scientists. Carter took his work quite seriously and dedicated his life to it. Carter's hard work, intelligence, and determination led to his discovery of Tutankhamun. The names of Carter and the boy king became forever linked.

CARTER'S TEAM Carter's work ethic rubbed off on the talented people who helped him find and catalog Tutankhamun's tomb in the Valley of the Kings. Among them were experts from the British Museum in London and the Metropolitan Museum of Art in New York City.

> *"It was our great privilege to find the most significant collection of Egyptian antiquities that have ever seen the light of day."*
> Howard Carter

Zahi Hawass (1947-)

Former Egyptian Minister of Antiquities Zahi Hawass is world renowned for his work in Egyptology. He has directed excavations at numerous ancient sites and has made his own significant discoveries. In 2005, Hawass directed a project that briefly removed Tutankhamun's **mummy** from the tomb. A **computed tomography (CT)** scan provided remarkable detail of Tutankhamun's physical body as well as a likely cause of death.

DEDICATION For more than 30 years, Hawass has worked to restore the treasures of ancient Egypt—dispersed in museums around the world—to their country of origin.

Nefertiti: The Great Royal Wife

Nefertiti, one of the most famous women of ancient Egypt, was the Great Royal Wife (the king's main wife) of Akhenaten. She gave birth to six daughters, including Ankhesenamun, who became Tutankhamun's wife. Most historians believe Nefertiti had an active role during the reign of Akhenaten. Nefertiti supported Akhenaten's religious conversion, and added Neferneferuaten *(Beautiful are the Beauties of Aten)* to her name. Many historians believe she ruled Egypt at some point between Akhenaten's death and the accession of young Tutankhamun.

The reign of Akhenaten and Nefertiti is called the *Amarna Revolution* because of the many changes they made in art, religion, and social practices. Amarna art depicts Akhenaten with exaggerated features and feminine hips. Nefertiti underwent a series of changes in Amarna art. She transformed from a unique beauty to an almost mirror image of Akhenaten (as in the stone **relief** at right), and back again (as shown in the famous bust below).

The great consistency of Amarna art lies in the repeated placement of Akhenaten and Nefertiti side-by-side, with equal stature. This represents a high regard for the queen, a fairly equal division of power, and a strong bond between the two. No other ancient Egyptian king and queen were depicted together with such frequency.

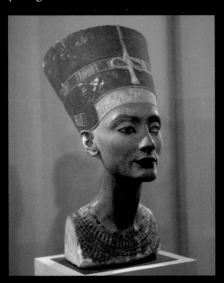

BUST OF NEFERTITI

Nefertiti, whose name means *the Beautiful One Has Arrived,* is indeed remembered for her beauty. Her famous bust, found at Amarna in 1912, is one of ancient Egypt's greatest art treasures. The bust, created around 1340 B.C., is limestone and painted stucco covered with transparent gypsum. The right eye is inlaid with crystal with a black wax pupil. The blank left eye was never finished.

The Younger Lady

In 1898, the mummies of a young boy and two women were found together in a tomb in the Valley of the Kings. There was much speculation about their identities, but nothing could be proven. More than 100 years later, **DNA** comparisons with positively identified mummies showed the "older lady" to be Tiye,

mother of Akhenaten (and grandmother of Tutankhamun). DNA tests showed the unnamed "younger lady" to be Tiye's daughter, Akhenaten's sister, and Tutankhamun's mother. The boy's identity remains unknown. Historians think the mummies were moved in a rush from Amarna to Thebes.

THE ROYAL FAMILY

Akhenaten, *at left,* and Nefertiti play tenderly with three of their daughters on this limestone house altar. The sun god Aten, represented by the disc at the top of the carving, reaches out with his many hands to caress the royal family. The fluid curves of the relief are typical of Amarna art.

ANCIENT MURDER

The **mummy** of Tutankhamun's mother, known only as the "younger lady," shows a terrible wound to the face. Historians believe she was violently murdered.

his arm into the darkness. His diary recorded the moment: "as my eyes grew accustomed to the light, details of the room within emerged slowly from the mist, strange animals, statues, and gold—everywhere the glint of gold." Lord Carnarvon broke the silence, anxiously asking Carter, "Can you see anything?" Carter, dazzled by the shining gold, responded, "Yes, wonderful things!"

That door opened into an **antechamber,** then an open room bursting with extraordinary objects. It was in a disorderly state, evidence of a frustrated or small-scale robbery in ancient times. Perhaps items were missing, but so much remained, thousands of wonderful things, and most bore the name or likeness of the boy pharaoh Tutankhamun.

After opening other sealed doorways, Carter at last entered the burial chamber on Feb. 17, 1923. The room contained a golden shrine and dazzling paintings on the walls and ceilings. Another room to the side was packed floor to ceiling with random treasures. Within the golden shrine lay the **sarcophagus** of Tutankhamun. With great care and effort, the sarcophagus was opened, revealing three nested (one inside the other) coffins, two of gold-plated wood, and a final one of solid gold. Inside, a gold funerary mask covered the face and shoulders of a mummy wrapped in linen cloth. It was Tutankhamun. Carter and Carnarvon had found the 62nd and final royal tomb in the Valley of the Kings.

The Valley of the Kings

The Valley of the Kings is a rocky, narrow *gorge* (steep valley) that was used as a cemetery by the rulers of ancient Egypt between 1545 and 1075 B.C. The valley lies on the west bank of the Nile River across from Luxor (ancient Thebes). Over 60 tombs have been discovered in the Valley of the Kings and in the adjoining Western Valley.

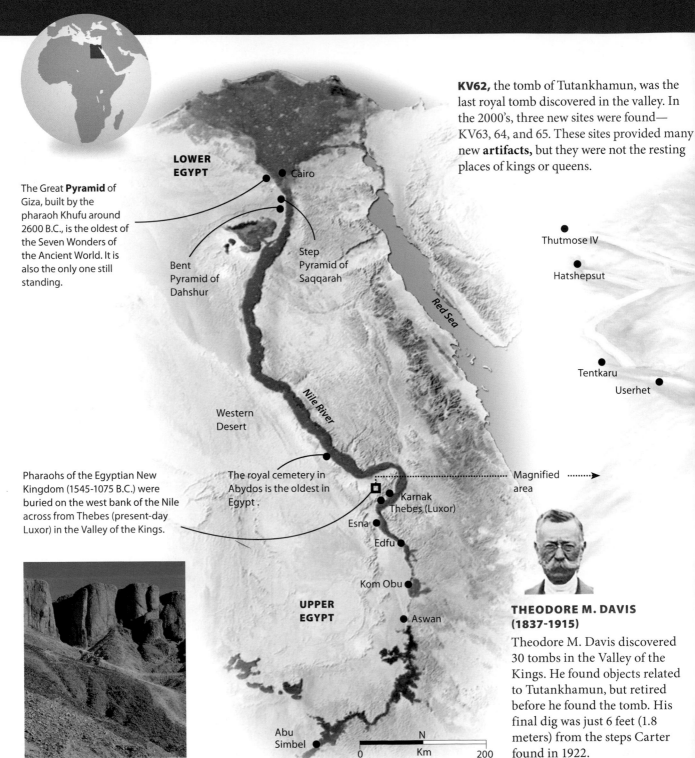

KV62, the tomb of Tutankhamun, was the last royal tomb discovered in the valley. In the 2000's, three new sites were found— KV63, 64, and 65. These sites provided many new **artifacts,** but they were not the resting places of kings or queens.

The Great **Pyramid** of Giza, built by the pharaoh Khufu around 2600 B.C., is the oldest of the Seven Wonders of the Ancient World. It is also the only one still standing.

LOWER EGYPT

Cairo

Bent Pyramid of Dahshur

Step Pyramid of Saqqarah

Red Sea

Thutmose IV

Hatshepsut

Tentkaru

Userhet

Nile River

Western Desert

Pharaohs of the Egyptian New Kingdom (1545-1075 B.C.) were buried on the west bank of the Nile across from Thebes (present-day Luxor) in the Valley of the Kings.

The royal cemetery in Abydos is the oldest in Egypt .

Magnified area

Karnak
Thebes (Luxor)

Esna

Edfu

Kom Obu

UPPER EGYPT

Aswan

THEODORE M. DAVIS (1837-1915)

Theodore M. Davis discovered 30 tombs in the Valley of the Kings. He found objects related to Tutankhamun, but retired before he found the tomb. His final dig was just 6 feet (1.8 meters) from the steps Carter found in 1922.

Abu Simbel

N

0   Km   200

KV62

Each major site in the Valley of the Kings is assigned an Egyptological *designation* (describing title). King Tut's tomb is designated KV62. *KV* stands for *King's Valley,* and *62* tells us it was the 62nd site found in the area.

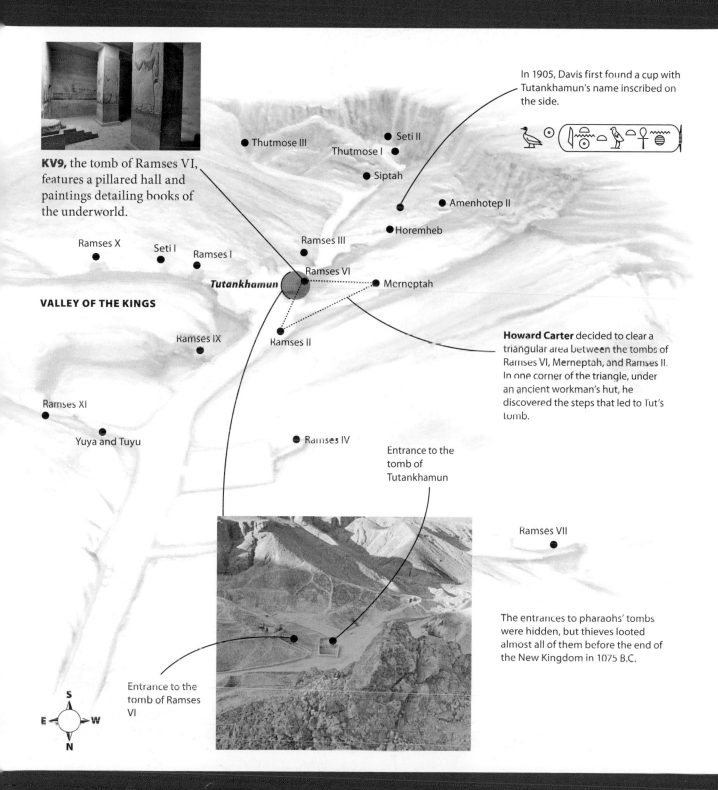

KV9, the tomb of Ramses VI, features a pillared hall and paintings detailing books of the underworld.

In 1905, Davis first found a cup with Tutankhamun's name inscribed on the side.

Thutmose III

Thutmose I

Seti II

Siptah

Amenhotep II

Horemheb

Ramses X

Seti I

Ramses I

Ramses III

Ramses VI

Tutankhamun

Merneptah

VALLEY OF THE KINGS

Ramses IX

Ramses II

Howard Carter decided to clear a triangular area between the tombs of Ramses VI, Merneptah, and Ramses II. In one corner of the triangle, under an ancient workman's hut, he discovered the steps that led to Tut's tomb.

Ramses XI

Yuya and Tuyu

Ramses IV

Entrance to the tomb of Tutankhamun

Ramses VII

The entrances to pharaohs' tombs were hidden, but thieves looted almost all of them before the end of the New Kingdom in 1075 B.C.

Entrance to the tomb of Ramses VI

The Tomb of Tutankhamun

King Tut's tomb, which is much smaller than the tombs of other pharaohs, was meant for someone else. Tutankhamun died suddenly, and at a quite young age. The tomb intended for him was no doubt under construction, but it wouldn't be ready for many years. A finished tomb in the Valley of the Kings was chosen, and converted quickly to accommodate the boy king.

Pharaoh's luck

Some 200 years after Tutankhamun's tomb was sealed and hidden in the Valley of the Kings, the tomb of Ramses VI was excavated almost on top of it. The rubble and debris from that work left Tut's tomb covered and lost to history for over 3,000 years.

Annex
Behind the furniture, a hidden entrance led to an adjacent room. Like an overstuffed modern closet, the annex was crammed with a variety of items.

Entrance
Howard Carter found the first step leading down into the tomb's entrance in 1922. Armed guards protected the entrance while the tomb was explored and its contents were catalogued.

Antechamber
Hidden doors in the *antechamber* (front room) led to other parts of the tomb. Carter's first glimpse of the room revealed "wonderful things."

5 ft 6 in

6 ft 6 in

Off the burial chamber, behind an open door, was the Treasury. A statue of Anubis, god of mummification, guarded the entrance and four goddesses protected the canopic shrine.

The canopic shrine held four coffin-shaped jars which contained some of Tut's organs. The liver, lungs, stomach, and intestines were removed from the body to keep them from decomposing inside of the **mummy.**

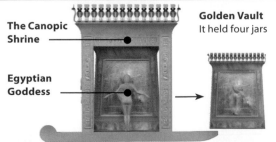

The Canopic Shrine

Egyptian Goddess

Golden Vault
It held four jars

Jar   Organs

Why the Mess?

A large number of *funerary* (burial) items were crammed into the tomb's four small rooms. In ancient times, thieves had broken into the tomb. Their hurried search for the most valuable items left things in a jumble. The fact that so much treasure still remained, however, shows that the thieves were interrupted, or were prevented from returning. The tomb was resealed and, much to the benefit of Howard Carter and the rest of the world, untouched until modern times.

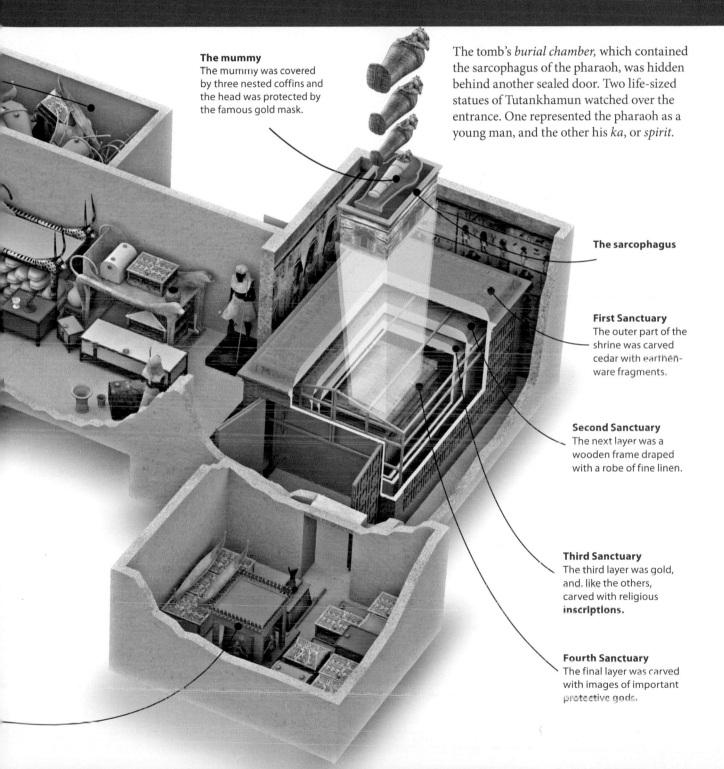

The mummy
The mummy was covered by three nested coffins and the head was protected by the famous gold mask.

The tomb's *burial chamber,* which contained the sarcophagus of the pharaoh, was hidden behind another sealed door. Two life-sized statues of Tutankhamun watched over the entrance. One represented the pharaoh as a young man, and the other his *ka,* or *spirit.*

The sarcophagus

First Sanctuary
The outer part of the shrine was carved cedar with earthen-ware fragments.

Second Sanctuary
The next layer was a wooden frame draped with a robe of fine linen.

Third Sanctuary
The third layer was gold, and, like the others, carved with religious **inscriptions.**

Fourth Sanctuary
The final layer was carved with images of important protective gods.

The Burial Chamber

King Tut's **mummy** lay within three nested coffins, a sarcophagus, and a multilayered shrine in the burial chamber. On the north wall of the chamber, a painted mural depicts—from right to left—the pharaoh's journey into the afterlife. The burial chamber is the only room of the tomb that is painted, further proof of the rush that surrounded Tutankhamun's burial.

3 **AFTERLIFE**

Writing and images in English are read from left to right. These images from Tutankhamun's tomb, however, are viewed from right to left—resurrection, deification, afterlife.

Adorned with his *nemes* (the headgear that identified him as a pharaoh), Tutankhamun (center) is embraced by Osiris (far left) in

the underworld. Behind the pharaoh is his *ka*, or essential spirit, in the form of a twin (far right).

before the paint was dry—another sign of a hurried burial. The damp paint combined with the warmth, darkness, food offerings, and recently mummified pharaoh to create an ideal environment for mold growth.

The "Pharaoh's Curse"

Mysterious deaths followed the fantastic discovery of Tutankhamun's tomb. Some people blamed the deaths on an ancient curse dooming anyone who disturbed a pharaoh's tomb. Newspapers called it the "pharaoh's curse."

Lord Carnarvon was in poor health near the end of the search for the tomb of Tutankhamun. In early March 1923, a few months after finding the tomb, a mosquito bite on Carnarvon's cheek became infected. The infection quickly led to blood poisoning, pneumonia, and, on April 5, his death. With so much attention already on the discovery of Tutankhamun, Carnarvon's sudden death caused wild speculation. Some newspapers—hoping to outsell their rivals—pushed the idea of a curse protecting the sacred tombs of the pharaohs.

The idea of a "pharaoh's curse" was not a new one. One old legend warned that mummies could return to life and attack tomb raiders. In the 1800's, riding the wave of Egyptomania, several stories and tales described the horrors of a **mummy's** curse.

As for the ancient Egyptians themselves, there were no curses written in the tombs. A number of ancient walls, however, warned potential thieves of divine punishment—or death by such animals as crocodiles or snakes. The Egyptians were more focused on the royal person being buried in the tomb. The walls often describe the royal journey into the afterlife, a sort of road map for the pharaoh's spirit. "Quotes" of tomb curses in the newspapers were either entirely made up or impossible to verify.

EVENTS BLAMED ON THE CURSE

The lack of actual curses did not stop the sensational belief in them. Carnarvon's death was followed by other "cursed" events such as the disappearance of his pet canary. Some news reports claimed a cobra—a royal symbol and an animal sacred to the ancient Egyptians—devoured the bird in its cage. Carnarvon, however, apparently gave the bird away for safe keeping. At around the same time Carnarvon died, his dog died in the United Kingdom and the lights went out in Cairo—events blamed on the "pharaoh's curse."

Over the next 10 years, 6 of the 26 people present at the opening of Tut's funeral chamber were dead. This was not an alarming death rate for a group of professional people mostly in their 40's and 50's in 1922, particularly for people living and working in Egypt's largely unsanitary conditions at the time. They were probably safer inside the tomb than out!

Somehow, Howard Carter—surely the curse's number one target—escaped death until 1939, just missing his 65th birthday. And there is no record of the curse striking down any the millions of tourists who have visited ancient Egyptian sites before or since the discovery of Tutankhamun's tomb.

FATAL MOSQUITO BITE

A mosquito bit Lord Carnarvon shortly after he first entered Tut's burial chamber in late February 1923. The next day, while shaving, he opened the wound and it became infected. He died just a few weeks later. *At left* is his death certificate and the razor blade that caused the infection.

Matching marks

The infected mosquito bite on Lord Carnarvon's cheek left a significant wound on the left side of his face. Two years after his death, rumors and theories fuelled the legend of the curse after Tutankhamun's mummy was first examined. Tut's left cheek bore a mysterious mark in the same exact spot as Lord Carnarvon's wound.

Lord Carnarvon

The curse in the press

To help finance the work on King Tut's tomb, Lord Carnarvon sold exclusive rights to the story to the *London Times*. This angered competing newspapers around the world, particularly a London *tabloid* (pictorial newspaper) called the *Daily Mail*. Short on information and desperate to compete with the Times, the *Daily Mail* (as well as many other newspapers) played up the legend of the curse. In the months and years following Carnarvon's death, the press compiled a list of some 30 deaths supposedly related to the "pharaoh's curse," the "curse of Tutankhamun," or the "revenge of the pharaohs," depending on the article. The superstitious and sensational stories did not sit well with Howard Carter, who repeatedly denied any connection between modern events and mystical curses of the past. Still, the legend lived on, leading to numerous books and movies and even the fear of mummies already in museums.

Responsible newspaper articles about Tutankhamun, however, informed the reading public on an endlessly intriguing topic. They also greatly increased people's knowledge of ancient Egypt and introduced many to the difficult science of archaeology.

Arthur Conan Doyle
(1859-1930)

Doyle, creator of the fictional detective Sherlock Holmes, believed the dead could communicate with the living. He thought that ancient priests had created "elementals" (curses) to protect Tutankhamun for eternity.

Marie Corelli
(1855-1924)

In a 1923 newspaper article, popular British novelist Marie Corelli stirred emotions and imaginations by quoting an ancient Arabic text stating that the "most dire punishment follows the rash intruder into a sealed tomb."

Walter Hauser
(1893-1959)

American architect Walter Hauser assisted Howard Carter and drew the floor plan of Tutankhamun's tomb. Curse or no curse, Hauser worked long hours in the tomb and lived 37 years after its opening.

The Death of Tutankhamun

X rays of Tutankhamun revealed a number of broken bones, spawning numerous theories on his death. In 2005, a three-dimensional **computed tomography (CT)** scan provided much more evidence, and scientists think they now know what killed the boy pharaoh more than 3,300 years ago.

Tutankhamun's **mummy** was first examined on Nov. 11, 1925. Howard Carter, British doctor Douglas Derry, and Egyptian doctor Saleh Bey Hamdi performed the examination. Oils and resins used during mummification caused the mummy's linen bandages to stick together, and the mummy itself was stuck to the bottom of the coffin as well as to the golden funerary mask. With great difficulty, the linens were unwrapped. To move Tut's mummy, then, Carter's team was forced to cut the body down the middle and remove the arms and legs. Freed from the coffin, the mummy was examined, measured, and photographed. The team concluded that Tutankhamun was between 17 and 19 years old when he died, and he stood 5 feet 6 inches (1.7 meters) tall. The team noted broken fragments in the pharaoh's skull and a lesion on the left cheek. Despite the carbonized appearance of the head, Carter made the poetic note: "face of an adolescent, noble, with beautiful features …"

X RAYS AND CT SCAN

In 1968, British doctor Ronald G. Harrison X-rayed Tutankhamun inside his tomb. He found the same bone fragments in the skull, giving rise to speculations of murder. Harrison also noted that the sternum and a large portion of the king's ribs were missing. The X rays showed a serious fracture in the pharaoh's left *femur* (thigh bone), but it was unclear if the injury occurred before or after death. American doctor J. E. Harris performed another set of X rays in 1978, this time to study the pharaoh's teeth.

In 2005, archaeologist Zahi Hawass led an Egyptian team that removed the mummy from the tomb. Swiss anatomist Frank Rühli, Austrian pathologist Edward Egarter, and Italian radiologist Paul Göstner then performed a CT scan on Tutankhamun. After studying the CT scan's 1,700 images, they unanimously agreed: Tutankhamun was not murdered. So what killed him?

Although they can't be sure, scientists think that Tutankhamun most likely died from complications related to his broken leg. Numerous guesses for the fracture's cause have included a chariot accident, a battle wound, even the vicious bite of a hippopotamus. But Tut suffered from foot deformities, which would have limited his mobility. He probably did not ride in chariots or fight in battles or even swim in the hippo-infested waters of the Nile. Scientists think the intermarriage with close relatives practiced by Egyptian royals caused Tut's foot problems, as well as other health problems, including **epilepsy.** A violent seizure, then, could have resulted in a fall, breaking the leg. Such a serious wound could easily have become infected. With no medicines to fight such an infection, it could have killed King Tut.

Blame it on the embalmers

Bone fragments in Tutankhamun's skull led some to believe that he had been killed by a blow to the head. Detailed CT scan images, however, traced the fragments to a fracture of the first cervical vertebra and the opening in the lower skull. Renowned Swiss doctor Frank Rühli, who participated in the CT scan, believes the injuries were caused by the **embalmers** after the king's death. He suspected Tut's sternum and front ribs were cut out to ease the removal of his internal organs. A hole in the lower skull was also most likely the work of the embalmers. Rühli is head of the Swiss **Mummy** Project, which uses modern scientific technology to study human differences, causes of death, and the evolution of disease in ancient mummies.

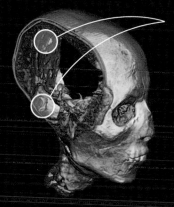

Loose bone fragments most likely came from a vertebra broken during the mummification process.

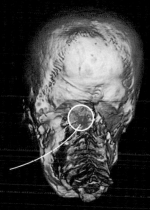

A hole in the lower skull was probably made by those responsible for removing the brain prior to mummification.

Bad break

The CT scan showed embalming fluid had leaked into the fracture in King Tut's leg. This means that the wound was open when he died. Whatever caused the break, the wound could easily have become infected, leading to Tut's premature death.

A mural shows Tut hunting from a chariot, something difficult to do with his foot deformities. His leg was thus probably not broken in a chariot accident.

ZAHI HAWASS supervised the CT scan in 2005.

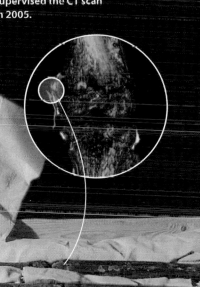

The Royal Funeral

Tutankhamun's funeral would have been an elaborate affair with **rituals,** a procession, and a feast. His sudden death, however, caused the burial preparations to be done in a rush. The king's tomb as well as many of the funerary items were meant for someone else. Even the **sarcophagus** and one of the coffins appear to have been made for someone else. The seasonal selection of flowers in the tomb showed the funeral probably took place in early spring.

The **viscera** (organs) were transferred in the canopic shrine. The brain was taken out and thrown away as having no value.

ANKHESENAMUN

Tut's Great Royal Wife and half-sister was one of the most prominent figures in the funeral procession. She was several years older than Tutankhamun. She later married Tut's closest advisor, Ay.

AY

The adviser and successor of Tutankhamun officiated as head priest and led the pilgrimage to Tutankhamun's final resting place.

Boating in the Afterlife

This model boat was found in King Tut's tomb. Ancient Egyptians believed boats transported gods through the heavens, an indication of the importance of the Nile River. New Kingdom pharaohs were carried in funerary boats toward their final home in the Valley of the Kings.

The Funeral Procession

The procession was led by the successor to the pharaoh, Ay, followed by members of the royal family, then the army generals and the high officials of the court. The procession departed from the temple of the city of Thebes and ended across the Nile in the Valley of the Kings. Despite the size of the procession, the specific location of the tomb was kept completely secret to protect it from potential thieves.

THE MOURNERS

A group of women who surrounded the main group, crying and wailing over the death of the pharaoh, were part of the ceremony.

THE SARCOPHAGUS

The **mummy** was transported inside the sarcophagus. Once inside the tomb, it was removed so as to perform the last rites before being laid to rest in the burial chamber.

SERVANTS AND SLAVES

They carried the supplies for the tomb and hauled the sarcophagus and the canopic shrine.

Did Tutankhamun Really Govern?

Tutankhamun became pharaoh as a young boy and died soon after he came of age. Ay, his grand *vizier* (minister of state), and Horemheb, the commander of the army, ran Egypt in Tut's youth and after his death. Did the boy king ever have any real power?

Around 1332 B.C., the son of Akhenaten was proclaimed pharaoh under the name Tutankhaten. He was just eight or nine years old. Government, military, and religious affairs, left in a state of turmoil by Akhenaten, needed the guiding hands of experience. Tut's chief advisor, Ay, probably took care of most of Egypt's internal affairs, while Horemheb dealt with Egypt's neglected borders and foreign policy. Both powerful men worked for the restoration of the state's *polytheistic* (worship of many gods) religion. Akhenaten had made Aten the only god of Egypt. This had angered many Egyptians, particularly Horemheb and the powerful priests devoted to the traditional chief god, Amun.

When Tut was about 13, Egypt's powerful elite forced the restoration upon the young pharaoh and reversed Akhenaten's reforms. They renounced Aten and returned Amun to the center of religious life. This was reflected in the pharaoh's name change from Tutankhaten to Tutankhamun as well as the return of the capital from Amarna to Thebes.

All this does not mean, however, that Tutankhamun had no power. As pharaoh, he still held the lives of all Egyptians— including Ay and Horemheb—in his hands. Being so young, however, and aware of his nation's problems, he relied heavily on the advice and influence of his court. He probably went along with Ay and Horemheb's return to the old ways, considering it the best thing for his kingdom.

Tut's death so soon after reaching maturity prevented him from accomplishing much of his own design. After he died, Ay and Horemheb ruled as pharaoh one after the other. Because of their connections to the religious reforms, Horemheb removed the names of Akhenaten, Tutankhamun, and Ay from Egyptian temples and texts.

A GOLDEN SHRINE

A detail from the Golden Shrine of Tutankhamun that depicts King Tut with his queen, Ankhesenamun, who puts fragrant oil on him in a ceremony.

Grand Vizier Ay and Horemheb

The family history of Ay is a bit confusing. He was probably the brother of Queen Tiye (Akhenaten's mother) and father of Nefertiti. This made him Tutankhamun's great-uncle and grandfather-in-law after Tut married Nefertiti's daughter, Ankhesenamun. Ay played a large role in Tutankhamun's life and later presided over the funeral of the young pharaoh. Ay then married Ankhesenamun (his granddaughter and grandniece) and took the throne as pharaoh himself. Horemheb (the statue on the right) is unusual for a ruler, in that he was not related to anyone from Tut's family. Nevertheless, Horemheb became pharaoh after Ay's death.

Grand Vizier Ay

Horemheb

The Pharaoh's Face

A team of archaeologists examined the results of a **computed tomography (CT)** scan of the **mummy** of Tutankhamun in 2005. This provided insights into what the face of the pharaoh Tutankhamun may have looked like in life.

Advanced technology

In 1972, 50 years after the great discovery of the tomb of Tutankhamun by **Egyptologist** Howard Carter, medicine witnessed one of the greatest advances of all time in the field of radiology. In that year, computed tomography was introduced. A few years later, in 1979, CT won its inventors the Nobel Prize in medicine. Instead of taking a single X-ray image (as does conventional radiography), tomography takes many, and as a result provides a cross-sectional image of a body part. In 1972, a scanner was invented to do the job digitally and process the results with a computer. In 1996, the volume generation technique was created to obtain 3-D images. This is the technology that was used in early 2005 to examine the mummy of the unfortunate Tutankhamun. The scan only took 15 minutes, but the analysis took several months. The mummy had already been X-rayed twice: first in 1968 and then in 1978. Computed tomography, designed to detect ailments in living patients, proved to be an invaluable tool for bringing the past to life.

THE SKULL IN DETAIL
The king's head was scanned in increments of just 0.02 inches (0.05 centimeters) in order to see the greatest detail possible of its complex structure, to unravel the mystery of his death and learn if he suffered from *congenital disorders* (birth defects).

The color of his skin

While science has provided the chance to continually move closer to understanding the distant past, some limits have not yet been overcome. The pharaoh's skin color is still unknown to us. Restorers based the reconstruction on paintings and busts of Tutankhamun (left), as well as those of his close relatives. The skin tones of modern Egyptians were also used as a reference and an intermediate tone from among these tones was selected.

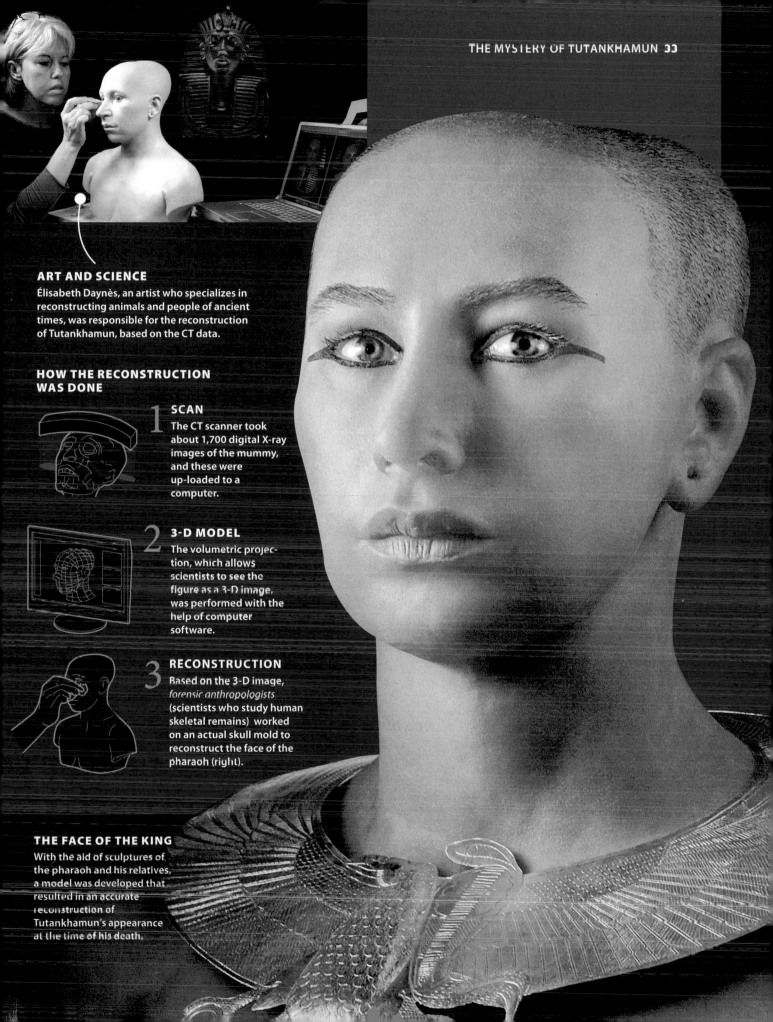

ART AND SCIENCE

Élisabeth Daynès, an artist who specializes in reconstructing animals and people of ancient times, was responsible for the reconstruction of Tutankhamun, based on the CT data.

HOW THE RECONSTRUCTION WAS DONE

1 SCAN

The CT scanner took about 1,700 digital X-ray images of the mummy, and these were up-loaded to a computer.

2 3-D MODEL

The volumetric projection, which allows scientists to see the figure as a 3-D image, was performed with the help of computer software.

3 RECONSTRUCTION

Based on the 3-D image, *forensic anthropologists* (scientists who study human skeletal remains) worked on an actual skull mold to reconstruct the face of the pharaoh (right).

THE FACE OF THE KING

With the aid of sculptures of the pharaoh and his relatives, a model was developed that resulted in an accurate reconstruction of Tutankhamun's appearance at the time of his death.

Mummifying the Dead

Ancient Egyptians mummified their dead to preserve the bodies for the afterlife. Embalmers prepared **mummies** by dehydrating the body. The complexity of the process depended on the wealth and status of the dead.

The earliest Egyptian mummies were naturally preserved by being buried in hot, dry desert sand. By about 3500 B.C., the Egyptians were experimenting with resin and linen wrappings to seal a dead body against moisture. By about 2600 B.C., they had developed a complicated process of preparing mummies that took 70 days to complete. In this process, the stomach, liver, lungs, and intestines—collectively known as *viscera* (VISS uhr uh)—were removed from the body through an incision on the left side of the abdomen. The heart, which the Egyptians considered the center of reasoning, was usually left in place. In some cases, **embalmers** removed the brain through the nose with a hook.

The body and organs were covered with *natron*, a powdery mixture of salt and sodium carbonate or sodium bicarbonate. This substance drew moisture out of the body tissues. After the body was dried, it was treated with perfumes and resins that helped seal out moisture. The body could be stuffed with straw, linen, moss, or other material to give it a more lifelike appearance. The body was then wrapped in a great number of linen bandages. Mummies were usually placed in a coffin or a series of coffins, one inside the other. The coffins were made of wood, stone, or precious metal and, in some periods, they were often shaped like the mummy and decorated.

Mummies in their coffins were buried in underground tombs. The internal organs were usually placed in the tomb in separate containers called *canopic jars*.

The Greek historian Herodotus (484?-425? B.C.) described Egyptian techniques of mummy preparation. Wealthy people could afford more elaborately prepared mummies than the poor. Ancient Egyptians also mummified animals, including baboons, cats, *jackals* (wild African dogs), and rams, which were associated with various Egyptian gods and cults. Pet cats and dogs were sometimes mummified after they died. The ancient Egyptians practiced mummification until about A.D. 300, when it was replaced by simple burials following the introduction of Christianity.

TUT'S MUMMY AND THE LITTLE ONES

As a dead pharaoh, Tutankhamun received the best and richest processes of mummification, which included a number of special bonuses. Within the linen wrappings of his mummy, a priest placed precious **amulets,** jewels, and other ornaments. Tut was also bathed in extra amounts of resin, giving his mummy a black appearance to match that of the powerful underworld god Osiris. And, of

Art in the chamber

The art in Tutankhamun's tomb is vastly different from the Amarna art of his father, Akhenaten. As with Akhenaten's religious reforms, the Egyptian elite wanted no part of his art reforms. The fluid lines and exaggerated features of Amarna paintings are largely gone, replaced by the rigid standards of earlier times. The "retro" artistic style carried over to the carvings, **reliefs,** sculptures, and other objects as well.

A mural on the funeral chamber's east wall shows Tut's shrine and sarcophagus on a ship carried by high dignitaries of the kingdom. They are ushering him into the afterlife. This was the first representation of a scene from the Book of the Dead in a royal tomb. The book is a collection of Egyptian religious maxims and other information to guide the soul on its journey to the underworld. Nearly all royal tombs after Tut feature scenes from the book as well.

On the chamber's west wall, another scene shows sitting baboons joyfully receiving the boat with two images of Osiris with a **scarab,** the symbol of resurrection and immortality. The mural on the north wall captured the most important ceremony of the funeral **ritual:** the opening of the mouth of the pharaoh, allowing him to move his lips to speak, eat, and breathe in the afterlife. The *Book of the Dead* included numerous spells, including one for the opening of the mouth ritual: "Awake! May you be alert as a living being, rejuvenated every day, healthy in millions of occasions of good sleep, while the gods protect you, with protection around you every day."

The mystery of the second-hand second coffin

King Tut's mummy was protected by the famous golden mask and three nested coffins. The inner coffin is pure gold, while the outer coffins are made of gold-covered wood. The face on the middle—or second—coffin *(below)* differs greatly from other representations of Tutankhamun. The second coffin, then, was no doubt intended for someone else. But no one knows who it is. Tut's stone outer **sarcophagus** showed signs that it, too, was built for a person other than the boy pharaoh.

Tutankhamun depicted as the god *Horus,* son of Osiris

These beautifully decorated stoppers topped Tutankhamun's coffin-like canopic jars.

course, Tut's **mummy** was laid to rest in costly coffins and shrines—even though they weren't all made specifically for him.

Tutankhamun and his wife Ankhesenamun tried at least twice to have a baby, but both pregnancies ended prematurely. The unfortunate babies—both daughters—were stillborn. The dead infants were still royal, however, and they were mummified just as their famous father would be shortly thereafter. The tiny baby mummies lay in their own miniature gold-plated nested coffins. The coffins were placed side-by-side in a wooden box in Tut's tomb treasury. Tutankhamun had no surviving children.

THE CANOPIC SHRINE

Tut's *viscera* (intestines, liver, lungs, and stomach) were extracted during **embalming.** However, like the mummified body, the organs were still needed by the pharaoh in the afterlife. Each organ, then, was placed in a canopic jar (or, in Tut's case, four miniature golden coffins)

for safekeeping. These "jars" were placed in a chest as part of Tutankhamun's magnificent canopic shrine found in the treasury. A gold-covered wooden sled holds the chest as well as four goddesses with arms outstretched to protect the king's viscera. The goddesses—Isis, Neith, Nephthys, and Selkis—are associated with the afterlife, mourning, mummification, and protection of the dead. The shrine is topped by cobras (royal symbols) with solar disks (symbolic of Ra, the sun god revived to replace Aten).

SPECIAL ITEMS OF THE TOMB

An altar encrusted in gold, silver, and decorative stones also stood in the treasury. The altar held a small coffin bursting with **amulets,** armor, jewelry, and vases used in Tut's funeral ceremony. The pharaoh, in the form of the jackal (or dog) god, Anubis, guarded this altar. A fleet of model ships lay scattered throughout the room, each for a leg of Tut's journey through the afterlife. (Boat scenes are shown in the funeral

chamber's wall paintings.) Hundreds of small wooden figurines called *ushabti* were also in the treasury. These gold-covered wooden figures represented Tut's many servants for the afterlife.

Many of the tomb's objects reveal the personal tastes of the young pharaoh. His enthusiasm for hunting and warfare is displayed in numerous items, including bows, arrows, boomerangs, daggers, and spears.

ANUBIS
A priest dressed as Anubis, the god of mummification, oversaw the entire process.

COMING BACK TO LIFE
Hathor, the goddess of the West, "where the sun sets," receives the dead king and revives him by bringing an ankh close to his nose. The ankh symbolized the generation of life. Behind the pharaoh is the god Anubis. The mural is located on the south wall of Tut's funeral chamber.

A wooden fan shows the pharaoh in a two-horse chariot during an ostrich hunt. A golden statue shows Tut as the god Horus hunting from a boat (shown on the previous page). Tut's physical limitations, however—particularly his foot deformities—probably prevented him from participating in many of these activities. But he no doubt still enjoyed watching them, much like modern sports fans of today.

One pastime Tut probably did actively play was a popular ancient table game called *senet*. An elaborate senet game board—double-sided panels of ebony and ivory on a panther-footed table—was found in the tomb, and mounted on a sled just like his canopic shrine. Known as "the game of passing," senet may have represented a challenge to gain access to the afterlife.

In 1922, when Howard Carter opened the tomb, the fragrance of lotus flowers and nightshade berries seemed to linger in the air. Harry Burton photographed a number of ancient flowers and plants from the tomb, but the delicate, dried petals and stems disintegrated when they were moved. Carter wrote of finding flowers on the mummy itself, a last offering, he believed, from the young king's grieving wife.

WRAPPING

The head was wrapped first. Then the left side was wrapped. Then the fingers and toes, arms and legs. The torso was wrapped last.

ORDER

The wrapping of the body was carried out after removing the viscera through an incision in the abdomen. The bandages closest to the body were coarser than the exterior ones.

AMULETS

Some 150 ornaments were wrapped within the linens of Tut's mummy. They included a **scarab** beetle made of black resin and gold cuffs sewn into the fabric around the mummy's wrists.

INCENSE

During the operation, incense was burned to perfume the air while the mummification work progressed as quickly as possible.

JARS

The viscera were placed in these jars, which usually had figures of protective gods. In the case of Tutankhamun, they were made in the shape of small coffins.

Why Were Tut's Treasures Left Behind?

Tutankhamun's tomb was found largely undamaged, but not completely. Thieves entered the tomb shortly after Tut's funeral over 3,000 years ago. Luckily, the robbers left many treasures behind, and they never reached the mummified pharaoh.

Until Howard Carter discovered Tutankhamun's tomb, ancient Egyptian royal tombs had been found largely robbed of their contents. The tombs were looted in the years soon after the funerals, when many people knew where to find them. Tutankhamun's tomb, too, was robbed shortly after the young pharaoh's death. Many of his funeral objects had been dismantled or tampered with, and they were missing such decorative gold and bronze fragments as arrowheads, buckles, joints, and staples. Ancient inventory lists found in the tomb showed that most of the tomb's oils, perfumes, and jewelry had been stolen. Many chests and jars had been overturned and emptied. Larger items, such as tables, benches, and chariot wheels, were left behind. And, most importantly, the thieves either ignored Tut's burial shrine or didn't have

enough time to break into it. The exquisite golden funerary mask would no doubt have been a profitable prize.

MAYA'S MEN

At the time of Tut's death, a powerful figure named Maya served as director of the royal treasury. It was his responsibility to protect the kingdom's riches, for both the living and the dead. Maya served Tut as well as the pharaohs Ay and Horemheb. It is thought that his agents—the royal authorities, so to speak—were the ones who foiled the robbery attempt and resealed Tut's tomb. The holes made by the raiders were plastered over and stamped with the seal of Anubis, guide to the afterlife, above the figures of nine bound thieves. As the locations of royal tombs were top secret, it is likely that the thieves had been members of Tut's large funeral procession.

Tomb raiders in Tut's time did not want to be caught. Captured thieves' feet were painfully beaten with sticks. They were then *impaled* (killed by being thrust upon sharpened stakes).

After the end of the New Kingdom in the 1070's B.C., the high priest of Amun (and later pharaoh) Pinedjem took steps to stop potential thieves. He cleared many royal tombs and combined treasures as well as mummies into common, more easily protected areas.

CAUGHT RED-HANDED?

Gold rings were found wrapped in this ancient linen scarf. It was likely dropped by thieves eager to escape Tut's tomb—and the authorities.

The sealed shrines

Tutankhamun's **mummy** was well-protected. It lay within three nested coffins, a **sarcophagus,** and four layers of shrines. The doors of the outer shrine, latched by sliding ebony bolts, was easily opened and closed. The doors of the next two shrines, however, were tied tightly with rope, and the ropes bore a clay royal seal. It would be impossible to open the shrines without destroying the seals. Whatever was inside, it most likely hadn't been touched for thousands of years.

Immensely excited, Howard Carter had Harry Burton carefully photograph the unbroken seals. For, just like ancient thieves, Carter's team would have to break them to open the shrine's doors. Carter was hesitant to cut the rope and seal and undo the sacred lock. But he had no choice and was forced to destroy to discover. Once opened, the shrines revealed Tut's sarcophagus, coffins, gold funerary mask, and the boy pharaoh himself.

Traces of theft

Tutankhamun's tomb showed evidence of two robberies. Holes had been dug (and then mostly resealed) in the plaster doors between each of the tomb's rooms. The diagram at right shows the various openings made by the looters. Several items were stolen from the tomb, and the remaining items lay somewhat scattered. The tomb was twice repaired and, thanks to construction rubble from later tombs, remained hidden for more than 3,000 years.

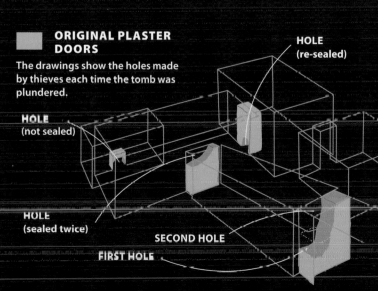

ORIGINAL PLASTER DOORS

The drawings show the holes made by thieves each time the tomb was plundered.

HOLE (not sealed)

HOLE (re-sealed)

HOLE (sealed twice)

SECOND HOLE

FIRST HOLE

The Pharaoh's Treasures

The items from Tutankhamun's tomb have a value to archaeologists that cannot be measured. They also have immense artistic and monetary value. Few archaeological discoveries in history have provided such mysterious and wonderful treasures.

The mask

The head and shoulders of Tutankhamun's mummy were covered by a carefully crafted mask of pure gold. Inlays of blue glass and semiprecious stones detail the mask. The priceless item is kept in the Egyptian Museum in Cairo, and its beauty still awes visitors from around the world. The mask is 21 inches (54 centimeters) tall and weighs about 24 pounds (11 kilograms). The forehead of the likeness of the monarch is adorned with a vulture and a cobra, royal symbols of both Upper and Lower Egypt. The mask, with the royal striped *nemes* (headdress) and a fine braided beard, represents Tut in the form of Osiris, god of the underworld. The mask is the most recognizable adornment of the mummy, but more than 100 other precious ornaments were also found on the body.

FANS

Elaborate fans—several of which were found in Tut's tomb—were carried by servants and used to help cool the pharaoh in Egypt's hot climate. This fan has inlays of ebony, decorative glass, and a thick gold coating. It was

The golden throne

An exquisite golden throne was the most impressive of the tomb's furnishings. The wooden throne is covered with gold, silver, and precious stones. Lion paws support the legs of the chair, and winged cobras form the armrests. The backrest contains a portrait of Tutankhamun with his wife, Ankhesenamun.

CROWN

Tut's mummy wore the royal crown, made of gold with inlays of semiprecious stones. The cobra and vulture decorations are removable and were found beneath the body.

CUPS

Howard Carter was fascinated by the odd shapes of the tomb's many cups, bowls, and vases. This drinking cup is in the shape of a lotus flower.

FIGURINES

A set of gold-covered wooden sculptures represented the pharaoh. These two wear the crowns of Upper and Lower Egypt.

ANUBIS

Anubis rests atop a shrine that held amulets, jewelry, and everyday items in Tut's tomb. Carved in wood and varnished with black resin, Anubis guards the shrine's

Places to See and Visit

OTHER PLACES OF INTEREST

THEBES

LUXOR, EGYPT

The city of Luxor is on the site of the ancient Egyptian capital of Thebes. Fantastic complexes and temples make Thebes the "world's greatest open air museum." The site includes the colossal ruins of the Karnak and Luxor temples.

EGYPTIAN MUSEUM

CAIRO, EGYPT

This is the most significant museum of ancient Egyptian culture in the world. The museum houses the treasures of Tutankhamun's tomb, except for the **mummy** itself, which is found in the original tomb in the Valley of the Kings. Tut's funerary mask is one of the most visited museum pieces in the world.

BRITISH MUSEUM

LONDON, UNITED KINGDOM

The British Museum's giant ancient Egyptian collection is world famous and includes the Rosetta Stone and Belzoni's famous bust of Ramses II.

The Valley of the Kings

The valley lies across the Nile River from Thebes, the ancient Egyptian capital. Many royal tombs in the valley, including that of Tutankhamun, can be visited (each for a small fee). In the western valley, only the tomb of Ay, Tutankhamun's successor, can be entered.

The valley is in a very hot region. Therefore, it is best to visit from October to March when the weather is cooler. Visitors should come prepared for rugged terrain and high temperatures. A hat, sunglasses, sunscreen, water, and good walking shoes are recommended.

A visit to three or four tombs in the valley can take most of a day. Not all of the tombs are open to the public, and those that are keep different hours according to the season. Tutankhamun's tomb is very small and modest. Therefore it is advisable to visit nearby tombs as well, such as the luxurious tombs of Ramses VI and Ramses III.

The Valley of the Queens

The tomb of Ramses II's great royal wife, Nefertari, and the temple of Queen Hatshepsut stand in a valley near the village of Deir el-Bahari close to the Valley of the Kings. Many New Kingdom queens and other royalty were buried in this valley.

METROPOLITAN MUSEUM OF ART

NEW YORK, NY, UNITED STATES

The "Met" has an extensive permanent collection of items relating to Tutankhamun and other ancient Egyptian royalty.

MUSEUM OF ANCIENT EGYPT

TURIN, ITALY

Turin's *Fondazione Museo delle Antichità Egizie* houses a substantial collection of Egyptian relics, including what is perhaps the oldest copy of the *Book of the Dead*.

NEUES MUSEUM

BERLIN, GERMANY

The Egyptian Museum of Berlin is located in the Neues Museum. It has a collection of high historical value, including the bust of Nefertiti and other works of ancient Egyptian art.

Glossary

Amulet— Charms, often worn around the neck, and used for protection.

Antechamber— a small room leading to a larger one.

Archaeology— The scientific study of the remains of past human cultures.

Artifact— Human-made objects.

Civilization— A society or culture that has complex social, political, and economic institutions.

Computed tomography— Or CT, an advanced type of X ray.

Cuneiform— An ancient writing system that used wedge-shaped letters.

Deity— A god or goddess.

Demotic— A simplified form of ancient Egyptian writing.

DNA—Chainlike molecules found in every living cell on Earth that direct the formation, growth, and reproduction of cells and organisms.

Dynasty— A series of rulers who belong to the same family.

Egyptologist— Scientist who studies ancient Egypt.

Embalm— To treat a dead body with spices, chemicals, or drugs to prevent decay.

Embalmer— A person who prepares dead bodies for burial or entombment.

Epilepsy— A chronic disorder of the nervous system.

Hieroglyphics— Pictures, characters, or symbols that stand for words, ideas, or sounds.

Inscription— Letters or symbols carved in such substances as clay or stone.

Mesopotamia— An ancient Middle Eastern civilization.

Mummy— A body that has been carefully preserved through natural or artificial means.

Obelisk— Great, upright, four-sided stone pillars.

Papyrus—A writing material made from the papyrus plant.

Phonetic—speech sounds and the symbols by which they are shown in writing and printing.

Pyramid— A structure with a square base and triangular sides meeting in a point.

Relief— Figures or designs that project from a surface in sculpture or carving.

Rituals— Religious ceremonies.

Sarcophagus— A stone coffin.

Scarab— A beetle sacred to the Egyptians.

Scroll— A roll of parchment, paper, or other material.

Viscera— The soft internal organs of the body.

Vizier— Advisor.

For Further Information

Books

Cox, Michael. *Tutankhamun and His Tombful of Treasure.*
London: Scholastic, 2012. Print.

Ganeri, Anita, and David West. *The Curse of King Tut's Tomb
and Other Ancient Discoveries.* New York: Rosen Pub.
Group, 2012. Print.

Hyde, Natalie. *King Tut.* New York: Crabtree, 2014. Print.

Lace, William W. *King Tut's Curse.* San Diego, CA:
ReferencePoint, 2013. Print.

Moore, Shannon Baker. *King Tut's Tomb.* Minneapolis:
Essential Library, 2014. Print.

Websites

"History: Tutankhamun (1336 BC - 1327 BC)." *BBC News.*
BBC, 2014. Web. 25 Feb. 2015.

"King Tut, Unraveling the Mysteries of Tutankhamun."
National Geographic. National Geographic, 2008. Web.
26 Feb. 2015.

"King Tut: Murder & Legend." *National Geographic Channel.*
National Geographic, 2014. Web. 26 Feb. 2015.

"Tutankhamen." *History.com.* A&E Television Networks,
2015. Web. 23 Feb. 2015.

"Tutankhamun, King of Egypt (1336-1327 BC)." *The British
Museum.* The British Museum, n.d. Web. 26 Feb. 2015.

Index

Acknowledgments

Pictures:

© Alamy Images

© AP Photo

© Bridgeman Images

© Corbis Images

© Getty Images

© Highclere Castle Archive (courtesy of the Earl of Carnarvon)

© iStockphoto

© Metropolitan Museum of New York Archives

© National Geographic Stock

© Science Photo Library

© The Griffith Institute Archive

© University of Oxford